RAW
CHOCOLATE

THE GOODNESS OF

RAW CHOCOLATE

40 AMAZING ANTIOXIDANT RECIPES

KATHY KORDALIS

PHOTOGRAPHY BY FAITH MASON

KYLE BOOKS

CONTENTS

A HISTORY OF CHOCOLATE

The cacao tree is thought to have been cultivated in Mesosamerica (roughly modern Central America) since 7000 BC, where it was significant in medicinal and ceremonial, as well as culinary, contexts. Indeed, so highly valued was it that the individual seeds were used by the Mayans and Aztecs as a form of currency.

The beans of cacao pods were used by the Mayans and Aztecs to make a bitter and rich drink, and it is believed that the word 'chocolate' is derived from the name of this drink, 'xocolatl', which means 'bitter water'.

Chocolate was introduced into Europe via the Spanish Court following the Spanish conquest. Although Europeans initially found it unpalatable, it became a very popular drink once sugar or honey and vanilla were added to sweeten it. With the Industrial Revolution, many aspects of food production became increasingly mechanised, and chocolate was no exception. Mass production and lower prices ensured that it became available to a much broader section of society.

In recent years, there has been a revival of interest in unprocessed whole foods and we are now rediscovering ways of the past in using raw cacao.

THE DIFFERENCE BETWEEN CACAO AND COCOA

There is no difference between a 'cacao tree' and a 'cocoa tree', nor between a 'cacao pod' and a 'cocoa pod' or a 'cacao bean' and a 'cocoa bean'!

In common parlance, the terms 'cocoa' and 'cacao' are often used interchangeably, but in this book, I use 'cocoa' to refer only to the resultant products from roasted beans, while 'cacao' describes the raw, unsweetened products of unroasted beans, which are used in my recipes.

For consistency, I also use 'cacao' botanically – after all, cacao is the main ingredient in chocolate, as well as the major provider of the associated health benefits!

DO THEY TASTE DIFFERENT?

Commercial, mass-produced chocolate is made from processed cocoa mixed with large amounts of sweeteners, dairy products and other flavourings. Raw cacao has a different flavour profile: it is stronger, with a much more pronounced bitterness, and lends itself exceptionally well to an array of recipes, both savoury and sweet. The recipes in this book will give you an excellent introduction to using raw cacao – very different from the flavours of mass-produced and highly processed chocolate products – and you can then use this delicious ingredient with confidence in other recipes.

What makes raw chocolate so special?

♦ Cacao contains a load of vitamins (B1, B2, B3, B5, B9, E) and minerals (particularly magnesium and manganese) and is packed with antioxidants (flavonoids), essential heart-healthy fat (oleic acid, a mono-unsaturated fat), protein and fibre.

♦ Cacao is believed to improve memory and mood, reduce the likelihood of heart disease, boost immunity and increase low-GI energy.

♦ Allowing the beans to naturally ferment instead of roasting them intensifies the berry and coffee flavours that are naturally found in raw chocolate.

♦ Raw chocolate is very versatile, works well in both savoury and sweet dishes and, most importantly, makes you feel good – body and soul!

Does cooked raw cacao retain its benefits?

A lot of misleading statements are made about the benefits of raw versus cooked foods in general. While cooking is needed to break down many vegetables into a form we can digest, and often releases additional nutrients, this is not necessary for cacao. Remember that unlike cocoa-based chocolate products, cacao has not been previously heated.

The recipes in this book require minimal cooking, ensuring that the cacao retains as many of its nutrients and their associated health benefits as possible. Even recipes where heating is required will be more nutritious than if made using the roasted cocoa equivalent.

THE BASICS

The main ingredients derived from cacao are beans, nibs, powder and butter. There are many ways to use these products, individually or in combination. In general, they are best mixed with something that has natural sweetness to balance the bitter taste.

Cacao Beans

A mature cacao tree will typically produce 20 pods a year, each one containing roughly 30 seeds – enough to make just 500g of chocolate.

Once harvested, the ripe cacao pods are cut open and the beans removed. The beans are then fermented, dried, cleaned and packed or processed further to produce cacao nibs, powder and butter.

Cacao Nibs

Once cacao beans have been fermented they are separated from their husks and broken into smaller pieces to form the cacao nibs. This happens during the process of winnowing the beans.

Cacao nibs contain roughly 58 per cent carbs, 14 per cent fat, an excellent source of protein (20 per cent) and fibre, making them a great component of shakes and smoothies. Their crunchy texture makes them great to use as a topping. They're also fantastic mixed with nuts and dried fruit, such as goji berries, as a snack.

Cacao Butter

The nibs are ground, then milled and the resultant liquor cold-pressed to unlock 75–90 per cent of the fat (cacao butter) content from the remaining protein, fibre and other solids. Cacao butter can be used in a similar way to other natural fats, such as coconut butter. Mix the right ratio of raw cacao and cacao butter to make your own delicious raw chocolate bars (see page 80).

Cacao Powder

The remaining solids form a cake, with 10–25 per cent of the fat remaining. This is then sifted through fine nylon, silk or wire mesh and used to make cacao powder. Cacao powder can be used instead of cocoa in traditional baking or added into a savoury dressing.

PRODUCTION & SUSTAINABILITY

There are three varieties of cacao tree from which beans are harvested: Criollo, Forastero and Trinitario, each with its own distinctive fragrance and flavour.

The most cultivated variety is the Forastero, accounting for 95 per cent of worldwide production. The Criollo is the original variety, native to Central and South America, and is considered the gold standard, as it is more aromatic and less bitter than the Forastero. However, it is very susceptible to disease, so cultivation is limited to just a few countries, most notably Venezuela. The Trinitario is a hybrid variety, similar in taste to the Criollo and slightly more hardy.

Cacao is primarily grown in West Africa, Southeast Asia and South America, all largely poor areas. The initial stages of production are very labour intensive. Most producers are on small-scale farms, who increasingly suffer from uncertainty as to the value of their crops, which are affected by disease, the effects of global warming and local political instability. In addition, the younger generation tends to move to local cities in search of an easier, more financially rewarding life.

By ensuring that the cacao products you buy are Fairtrade certified, you can exert a strong influence in ensuring that your consumption rewards these primary producers as much as possible. (Visit www.fairtrade.org.uk/en/farmers-and-workers/cocoa for more information.)

A growing number of 'bean-to-bar' craft chocolate makers are choosing to source their own cacao beans directly from selected farms. They then perform all the subsequent steps themselves, all the way through to the work of a fine chocolatier. Many of these chocolate makers sell through their own websites, through smaller retailers or at their own chocolate shops and cafés.

BREAKFAST & SNACKS

HOMEMADE GRANOLA & ROASTED FRUIT

*VEGETARIAN

This versatile granola, with the addition of puffed oats, can be eaten as a cereal, the base for a breakfast bar, or as a topping for yogurt or stewed fruit. Keep a jar of it at home and at work plus a little stash in your bag as a snack when you're on the run.

Serves 4-6
(granola makes a 1-litre jar)

For the granola
90g coconut oil, melted
2 teaspoons raw cacao powder, plus extra to serve
50ml maple syrup
70g puffed oats
60g unsweetened coconut flakes
100g mixed seeds
80g almonds, roughly chopped
50g chia seeds
Small pinch of salt
20g raw cacao nibs

For the Roasted Vanilla Rhubarb & Strawberries
200ml maple syrup
1 vanilla pod, halved and deseeded
50ml Cointreau (optional)
Pinch of sea salt
400g rhubarb, roughly chopped
300g strawberries, hulled and cut in half
4 strips orange peel

500g Greek-style yogurt, to serve

1. First, make the granola. This is best done a day or so in advance. Preheat the oven to 150°C/gas mark 2. Mix the coconut oil, cacao powder and maple syrup in a large bowl. Tip in all the remaining ingredients except the cacao nibs and mix well.

2. Tip the granola onto baking trays and spread out thinly and evenly. Bake for 15 minutes, then stir in the cacao nibs and bake for a further 5 minutes.

3. Remove from the oven and scrape onto a flat tray to cool. The granola can be stored in an airtight container for up to a month.

4. To roast the fruit, preheat the oven to 180°C/gas mark 4 and line a baking tray with greaseproof paper. In a small bowl, whisk together the maple syrup, vanilla seeds, Cointreau (if using) and salt. Put the rhubarb on the baking tray and pour over the syrup. Roast for about 15-20 minutes until tender.

5. Add the strawberries and orange peel and roast for a further 10 minutes. The juices should be thick and the rhubarb tender.

6. Remove from the oven and transfer to a bowl. Any leftovers will keep in an airtight container in the fridge for up to a week.

7. To serve, put two dollops of yogurt and 1 heaped tablespoon of granola in each of four or six bowls and top with the roasted fruits and juices and a sprinkling of raw cacao powder.

Look for a puffed oat that contains no added sweeteners or flavours, just 100 per cent wholegrain puffed oats. They become the perfect vehicle for any flavour!

SPICED CHOCOLATE & MAPLE BARS *VEGETARIAN *DAIRY-FREE

A perfect on-the-go bar packed with seeds, nuts and spiced raw chocolate. The sweetness of the rapadura (panela) sugar – an unrefined cane sugar with a light caramel flavour – balances the bitterness of the raw chocolate. Muscovado is a great alternative to rapadura sugar if you prefer; it imparts a similar caramel depth of flavour.

Makes 12

For the granola base
100ml maple syrup
2 tablespoons coconut oil
150g Homemade Granola
  (see page 14)
50g spelt flakes
3 tablespoons chia seeds
3 tablespoons flaxseeds
75g hazelnuts, chopped, half
  reserved for topping
75g pecans, chopped, half
  reserved for topping

*For the spiced
chocolate topping*
300g raw chocolate (80 per
  cent cacao), chopped
3 tablespoons coconut oil
1 tablespoon rapadura
  (panela) or muscovado
  sugar
1 teaspoon ground
  cinnamon
½ teaspoon ground ginger
20g unsweetened coconut
  flakes, toasted
10g raw cacao nibs

1. Preheat the oven to 180°C/ gas mark 4 and line a 20cm square baking tin with greaseproof paper.

2. To make the granola base, in a saucepan, combine the maple syrup and coconut oil and heat gently until melted. Add the granola, spelt flakes, chia seeds, flaxseeds and half the hazelnuts and pecans and stir to evenly coat all of the dry ingredients with the wet ingredients.

3. Pour the mixture into the prepared baking tin and use a spatula to spread into a thin, even layer. Bake for 15–20 minutes, or until golden in colour and the nuts smell toasty. Remove from the oven and leave to cool on a wire rack while you prepare the chocolate topping.

4. To make the topping, melt the chocolate in a bain-marie (a heatproof bowl placed over a pan of simmering water). Allow the chocolate to melt, stirring occasionally, then mix in the coconut oil, sugar, cinnamon and ginger.

5. Pour the melted chocolate mix over the baked granola base and spread into an even layer. While the chocolate is still wet, sprinkle evenly with the remaining nuts, the toasted coconut and cacao nibs.

6. Put in the freezer to set for 30 minutes, then break into pieces, or cut into 12 bars. They will keep in an airtight container in the fridge for up to a week.

TROPICAL FRUIT & NUT BARS *VEGETARIAN *DAIRY-FREE

Fruity and nutty, with the addition of cacao nibs and vanilla and almond flavours, these bars are great for breakfast but equally good as a snack at any time of day. With no refined sugars and all natural ingredients these are a good way to get a natural energy boost.

Makes 12

100g spelt flakes
50g each dried pineapple, mango and papaya, roughly chopped
50g dried physalis
40g macadamia nuts, roughly chopped
20g unsweetened coconut flakes
125ml brown rice syrup (or an equal mixture of honey and maple syrup)
4 tablespoons coconut oil
3 tablespoons almond butter
½ teaspoon almond extract (optional)
1 teaspoon vanilla extract
Pinch of ground cinnamon
1 teaspoon raw cacao powder
75g pitted medjool dates, blitzed to a paste in a blender
20g raw cacao nibs
20g ready-made chocolate-coated quinoa (optional)

1. Line a 20cm square baking tin with clingfilm and set aside. In a large bowl, combine the spelt flakes, dried fruits, macadamia nuts and coconut flakes.

2. In a saucepan, combine the rice syrup, coconut oil, almond butter, almond and vanilla extracts, cinnamon, raw cacao powder and blitzed dates and warm for 2–3 minutes, or until fully combined.

3. Pour this mixture over the dry mixture and stir together until combined. Put into the lined baking tin and use your fingers to press the mixture evenly into the tin. Sprinkle the cacao nibs and chocolate-coated quinoa (if using) evenly over the top and press down gently.

4. Put in the freezer to chill for 1 hour, then cut into 12 individual bars. They will keep in an airtight container in the fridge for up to a week.

If you can't source dried physalis, substitute it with a mixture of the other dried fruits.

COCONUT, CHERRY & CACAO NIB BARS

*VEGETARIAN *GLUTEN-FREE *DAIRY-FREE

My favourite chocolate bar when I was growing up in Australia was called a Cherry Ripe – dark chocolate filled with cherry coconut. This is a much more wholesome version, using real sour cherries and no refined sugars, with a nice balance of sweet, tart and bitter.

Makes 12

100g pitted Medjool dates
1 teaspoon vanilla extract
80g desiccated coconut
80g gluten-free oats
70g dried sour cherries
   (or use cranberries)
1 tablespoon raw cacao
   powder
70g coconut oil
1½ tablespoons maple syrup
30g dried barberries
   (optional), or use
   30g extra dried sour
   cherries or cranberries
20g raw cacao nibs
100g raw chocolate
   (80 per cent cacao),
   chopped

1. Line a 20cm square baking tin with clingfilm. Put the dates and vanilla extract into a food-processor and blend to a paste. Add the desiccated coconut, oats, half the sour cherries, the cacao powder, coconut oil and maple syrup and pulse until just combined but still with some texture.

2. Tip into a bowl and stir in the remaining cherries, the barberries and cacao nibs. Spoon into the prepared tin and freeze for 1 hour. Remove from the freezer and cut into 12 bars.

3. Melt the chocolate in a bain-marie (a heatproof bowl placed over a pan of simmering water), then drizzle the melted chocolate over the mixture in the tin. Alternatively, dip half a bar into the melted chocolate and place on a lined tray, then repeat for the remaining bars.

4. Place the tin or lined tray in the fridge to set, then wrap the bars. Once set and wrapped, they will keep in an airtight container in the fridge for up to a week.

RAW CHOCOLATE NUT & SEED SPREAD

*VEGETARIAN *GLUTEN-FREE *DAIRY-FREE

A nut butter with the added benefit of seeds, coconut oil and raw cacao powder. Not only are sesame seeds an excellent source of copper and a very good source of manganese, the addition of cashews and almonds also makes a protein-rich spread.

Makes a 400ml jar

For the Chocolate Sesame Seed Spread

200g sesame seeds
100g cashews
50g almonds
3 tablespoons coconut oil
2 tablespoons maple syrup
1 teaspoon vanilla paste
1 tablespoon raw cacao powder
Pinch of salt

For the Chocolate Hazelnut Spread

150g mixed seeds
200g hazelnuts
3 tablespoons coconut oil
2 tablespoons maple syrup
1 teaspoon vanilla paste
1 teaspoon raw cacao powder

1. Preheat the oven to 180°C/gas mark 4 and line a baking tray with greaseproof paper. Spread the seeds and nuts out on the tray and toast in the oven for 6–8 minutes.

2. Put the roasted seeds and nuts (reserving a quarter of the hazelnuts, if using) into a food-processor and process on high speed for 10–20 minutes (depending on the strength of your food-processor), stopping and scraping down the sides a few times.

3. When the mixture is smooth and creamy, add the remaining ingredients and blend until combined. If using hazelnuts, chop the reserved nuts and stir through.

4. Store in a sterilised glass jar in the fridge for up to 2 weeks.

POWERBALLS

ALL *VEGETARIAN *GLUTEN-FREE *DAIRY-FREE

Raw cacao helps lower the oxidative stress of strenuous activities because of the high levels of magnesium, chromium, B vitamins and antioxidants it contains, so these balls make a great snack after a workout. My husband likes to take them on a long bike ride to keep him going.

APRICOT, CASHEW & CACAO NIB

Makes 20

250g ready-to-eat dried apricots
200g cashews
2 tablespoons raw cacao powder, plus extra to dust
50g coconut oil, softened
20g raw cacao nibs

1. In a food-processor, blend the apricots, cashews, cacao powder and coconut oil into a paste. Add the cacao nibs and mix in well.

2. Form the mix into walnut-sized balls, put into a freezable container and place in the freezer. When ready to serve, remove from the freezer and dust with cacao powder. Defrost for 5–10 minutes before eating.

3. Powerballs can be kept in the fridge for up to 2 weeks after defrosting or in the freezer for up to 3 months.

For an extra hit of goodness, add 1 teaspoon of maca powder to any of these balls. Maca powder is derived from the maca root plant and plays an important role in increasing overall energy and vitality. Or you could add a scoop of protein powder.

DATE, FIG, COCONUT & GOJI BERRY

Makes 25

100g pitted Medjool dates
100g dried figs
100g raw almonds
50g coconut oil, softened
50g desiccated coconut
20g ground flaxseeds
1 teaspoon raw cacao
  powder
20g goji berries

1. Soak the dates and figs in a little water for 10 minutes, then drain.

2. In a food-processor, blend the dates and figs, almonds, coconut oil, desiccated coconut, flaxseeds and cacao powder into a paste. Stir in the goji berries and form the mix into walnut-sized balls. Put into a freezable container and place in the freezer. Defrost for 5–10 minutes before eating.

3. Powerballs can be kept in the fridge for up to 2 weeks after defrosting or in the freezer for up to 3 months.

ORANGE, HAZELNUT, DATE & MATCHA

Makes 20

300g hazelnuts
50g pitted dates, soaked in
  water for 10 minutes then
  drained
50g coconut oil
1 tablespoon raw cacao
  powder
Zest of 1 orange
1 tablespoon maple syrup
Pinch of salt
1 teaspoon matcha powder,
  plus extra to dust

1. In a food-processor, blend the hazelnuts, dates, coconut oil and cacao powder into a paste. Add the orange zest, maple syrup, salt and matcha powder and mix in well.

2. Form the mix into walnut-sized balls, put into a freezable container and place in the freezer. When ready to serve, remove from the freezer and dust with matcha powder. Defrost for 5–10 minutes before eating.

3. Powerballs can be kept in the fridge for up to 2 weeks after defrosting or in the freezer for up to 3 months.

RAW CHOCOLATE & BERRY SMOOTHIE

*VEGETARIAN *GLUTEN-FREE *DAIRY-FREE

Satisfy your sweet tooth with this healthy and delicious chocolate and berry smoothie: a no-guilt, feel-good-about-yourself treat! Berries are high in vitamin C and antioxidants, avocado is full of healthy fats, the dates make a great natural alternative to sugar, almond butter adds some protein, and raw cacao powder is high in magnesium, iron and flavonoids. Add a scoop of protein powder for a post-workout drink.

Serves 2

200g frozen or fresh
   mixed berries
½ avocado, peeled and
   stone removed
5 pitted Medjool dates
1 tablespoon almond butter
1 tablespoon raw cacao
   powder
300ml coconut or
   almond milk
Ice cubes (optional)

1. Place the mixed berries, avocado, dates, almond butter, cacao powder and coconut or almond milk in a blender and blitz until the mixture is smooth and silky.

2. Pour into two glasses and serve. Add some ice cubes for a colder smoothie, if you've used fresh rather than frozen berries.

SALTED CHOCOLATE
TOASTIE *VEGETARIAN *DAIRY-FREE

Inguldge in these toasties with oozy salted chocolate and dipped in maple syrup. Try it with the raw chocolate spreads on page 21 for alternative filling ideas.

Serves 4

8 slices good-quality
  seeded bread
4 tablespoons coconut oil
4 tablespoons crunchy
  hazelnut butter
100g raw chocolate
  (80 per cent cacao),
  broken into four
  equal-sized pieces
4 pinches of sea salt
Maple syrup, to serve
  (optional)

1. Heat a sandwich toaster or a small griddle pan. Spread each slice of bread on one side with the coconut oil.

2. Place four slices, oil-side down, onto some greaseproof paper or a plate. Spread each slice with 1 tablespoon of hazelnut butter, top with a piece of chocolate and sprinkle with a pinch of sea salt. Finish by topping each with the remaining slices of bread, oil-side up.

3. Place the four sandwiches into the sandwich toaster or onto the griddle pan. If you are using a sandwich toaster, press down and toast for 2–3 minutes. If cooking in a pan, squash down a little with the back of a fish slice while cooking, flip over after 1–2 minutes when golden, then cook on the other side.

4. Remove and set aside for 2 minutes to cool slightly, then cut each toasted sandwich into triangles or four fingers. Serve with a bowl of maple syrup to dip.

To make this toastie gluten-free, you can use your favourite gluten-free bread

CHOCOLATE-DIPPED FRESH FRUIT

*VEGETARIAN *GLUTEN-FREE *DAIRY-FREE

When I was growing up, a family feast would always finish with a large platter of fruit. This makes an impressive but light and healthy start to the day or a refreshing and non-guilt-inducing snack!

Serves 4

For the cinnamon chocolate
100g raw chocolate (80 per cent cacao), chopped
1 teaspoon honey
2 teaspoons ground cinnamon, plus extra to finish

For the goji coconut chocolate
100g raw chocolate (80 per cent cacao), chopped
1 teaspoon honey
10g unsweetened coconut flakes
10g goji berries, roughly chopped

For the fruit
2 passion fruits, halved
½ each small watermelon and small cantaloupe, peeled and cut into wedges
100g blueberries
100g raspberries
200g green grapes
200g purple grapes
8 strawberries
Zest of 2 limes, to decorate

1. Line a baking tray with greaseproof paper.

2. For the cinnamon chocolate, melt the chocolate with the honey in a bain-marie (a heatproof bowl placed over a pan of simmering water) until thick and smooth, then stir in the cinnamon and set aside.

3. For the goji coconut chocolate, melt the chocolate with the honey in a bain-marie until thick and smooth.

4. Divide all the fruit in half. With one half, dip each fruit halfway into the cinnamon chocolate, allowing the excess chocolate to drip off before placing carefully onto the lined baking tray.

5. Repeat with the other half of the fruits and the plain honey chocolate. While still wet, sprinkle half of these with coconut flakes and half with goji berries.

6. Place all the fruit in the fridge and allow the chocolate to set for at least 1 hour. Before serving, top the cinnamon chocolate-dipped fruit with a sprinkle of cinnamon, then decorate all the fruit with lime zest.

MAINS

ROASTED VEG WITH CHOCOLATE PICADA

Picada is a Catalan-style pesto traditionally made using almonds, but made here with hazelnuts, pine nuts, parsley and chocolate – a surprise ingredient that adds a pleasing touch of bitterness to this delicious side dish.

Serves 4

For the roasted veg

½ butternut squash, peeled, deseeded and cut into 1cm-thick half moons
1 small cauliflower, cut into florets
6 garlic cloves, unpeeled and bruised
500g golden beetroot, trimmed, scrubbed and cut into wedges
50ml olive oil
Pinch of celery salt
Black pepper

For the picada

150g hazelnuts
100g pine nuts
3 garlic cloves
A handful of flat-leaf parsley, leaves picked and roughly chopped
175ml olive oil
3 tablespoons sherry vinegar
Zest and juice of 1 lemon
1–2 tablespoons raw cacao powder, or to taste

1. Preheat the oven to 180°C/gas mark 4.

2. Put the prepared butternut squash, cauliflower, garlic and beetroot into a large roasting tray. Drizzle with the olive oil, sprinkle with the celery salt and ground pepper and mix, making sure that all the vegetables are well coated. Bake, uncovered, for 40–50 minutes, or until golden brown and just cooked.

3. Meanwhile, make the picada. Put the hazelnuts, pine nuts and garlic into a food-processor and pulse until you have a coarse texture. Tip the mixture into a bowl and mix in the parsley (reserving some to garnish), olive oil, sherry vinegar, lemon zest and juice and cacao powder to taste.

4. To serve, put the roasted vegetables on a serving dish, sprinkle with the reserved parsley and drizzle with some of the picada, serving the remainder in a bowl. This pesto can be stored in the fridge for up to 1 week.

Use purple beetroot if you can't get hold of golden. The picada is also delicious stirred through cooked quinoa and topped with some griddled chicken.

MEXICAN SHORT RIBS & PILONCILLO SAUCE

This dish, which has a great depth and balance of flavours, is all about slow-braising the short ribs until they're falling off the bone. It's a great dish to make ahead and freeze.

Serves 4

For the pickled onions
1 red onion, thinly sliced
Pinch of sea salt
1 teaspoon each whole black
   peppercorns, dried oregano
   and cumin seeds
3 garlic cloves, halved
250ml red wine vinegar

For the short ribs
2 onions, 3 carrots and
   3 celery sticks, quartered
3 garlic cloves
1 ancho or chipotle chilli
3 bay leaves
4–5 (1.5kg) beef short ribs
Juice of 1 lime
500ml beef stock or water

For the piloncillo sauce
40g blanched almonds
1 cinnamon stick
40g raw chocolate
   (80 per cent cacao)
¾ teaspoon rapadura (panela)
   or muscovado sugar
2–3 tablespoons smoked
   chilli paste (or to taste)

To serve
6–8 tacos, warmed
100g soured cream
Lime wedges
Coriander leaves

1. First make the pickled onions. In a bowl, toss the onion with the salt; let it sit for 15 minutes until it releases some of its liquid. Transfer to a sterilised jar and add the peppercorns, oregano, cumin and garlic. Pour over the vinegar and seal with a lid. Refrigerate for at least 4 hours before using. It will keep for up to 2 weeks in the fridge.

2. Preheat the oven to 180°C/gas mark 4. Put the onions, carrots, celery, garlic, chilli and bay leaves in a roasting tray. Arrange the beef short ribs on top, drizzle over the lime juice, pour over the stock or water and season with salt and pepper. Cover with foil and cook for 3–4 hours.

3. Meanwhile, for the piloncillo sauce, dry-toast the almonds and cinnamon in a frying pan over a medium heat, stirring frequently (5–6 minutes). Cool, set aside the cinnamon stick, then blend the almonds until finely chopped. Add the chocolate and sugar, blend until a chunky, crumbly mass forms, then set aside.

4. Remove the meat and vegetables from the oven and shred the meat from the bone. Set the meat aside in a warm place to rest for 15 minutes. Drain the braising liquid, reserving about 375ml, and discard the vegetables.

5. Pour the reserved braising liquid into a saucepan and add the Mexican smoked chilli paste and the reserved cinnamon stick. Bring to the boil, then reduce the heat to low and simmer for 5 minutes. Add the chocolate mixture and stir occasionally until the chocolate melts, then simmer until thickened, about 5 minutes. Strain the sauce through a sieve, or leave it chunky, then keep warm.

6. Arrange the shredded beef on a platter, pour over the sauce and serve with warmed blue or golden tacos, pickled onions, soured cream, and some lime wedges and coriander leaves.

CACAO BABA GANOUSH & CHILLI PITTA CRISPS

*VEGETARIAN *DAIRY-FREE

Raw cacao lends itself perfectly to the robust tang and earthy flavours of fire-scorched aubergine. As a great source of dietary fibre the aubergine comes in an array of colours. My preference is a mixture of solid purple and purple and white speckled skin, which is the source of many of its nutritional benefits, including potassium, magnesium and antioxidants. It is also very low in calories if you use a small amount of oil, as I do here.

Serves 4 as a side

3 aubergines
3 garlic cloves
Juice of 1 lemon
60g tahini
1 teaspoon raw cacao powder, plus extra for finishing
3 tablespoons olive oil, plus extra for brushing and drizzling
1 tablespoon pomegranate seeds
1 tablespoon roughly chopped parsley
1 spring onion, thinly sliced
Salt and pepper

For the chilli pitta crisps
6 mini brown pitta breads
½ teaspoon dried chilli flakes

1. Preheat the grill to high. Prick the aubergines with a fork, then grill until the skin is charred and blackened and the flesh feels soft when you press it (this will take approximately 15–20 minutes), turning halfway through cooking. Remove and set aside to cool.

2. For the chilli pitta crisps, split the pitta breads in half, brush the 'insides' with olive oil and cut each half into quarters. Arrange, cut sides up, on two baking trays. Sprinkle with salt, pepper and chilli flakes. Grill under a medium heat until golden and crisp, 10–12 minutes.

3. When the aubergines are cool enough to handle, cut them in half and scoop out the flesh. Put the aubergine flesh, garlic, lemon juice, tahini, cacao powder and olive oil in a food-processor and pulse until just combined for a coarser texture, or blend for longer if you prefer a smoother finish.

4. Put into a serving dish, drizzle over a little olive oil, season, then scatter over the pomegranate seeds, chopped parsley, spring onion and a pinch of cacao powder. Serve with the chilli pitta crisps.

BEEF, ALE & CHOCOLATE PIES

Warm your heart with these not-so-humble pies – a perfect remedy for winter blues! Plus recent studies have found unexpected benefits of ale and beer including vitamin B, fibre and stress reduction! Make them ahead of time and freeze for fuss-free serving. For some extra tang, top with Raw Chocolate BBQ Sauce (see opposite).

Serves 4

1 tablespoon olive oil
2 onions, chopped
600g braising steak, cubed
1 carrot, peeled and
   roughly chopped
2 celery sticks, roughly
   chopped
3 bay leaves
4 thyme sprigs, leaves
   picked
1 tablespoon tomato purée
300ml beef stock
300ml ale
2 tablespoons
   Worcestershire sauce
1½ tablespoons cornflour
2 teaspoons raw cacao
   powder
375g (2 sheets) ready-rolled
   all-butter puff pastry
1 egg, lightly beaten
Sea salt and pepper

1. To make the filling, heat the oil in a saucepan over a medium heat. Add the onions and cook for 10 minutes, or until soft. Add the meat and cook for 5 minutes, or until sealed and browned. Add the carrot, celery, bay leaves, thyme, tomato purée, stock, ale and Worcestershire sauce. Stir, then simmer gently, covered, for 2–3 hours, or until the meat is tender.

2. Preheat the oven to 190°C/ gas mark 5. Blend the cornflour, cacao powder and a little water to a smooth paste. Add to the beef mixture and stir for 4 minutes, or until the mixture has thickened and returned to a simmer. Season with salt and pepper, then set aside to cool.

3. Lay out one sheet of pastry on a lightly floured surface. Cut out four pie bases to line four 9cm pie tins. Line with greaseproof paper and fill with ceramic baking beans. Bake for about 15 minutes, or until the pastry is firm, then remove the beans and cook for a further 5 minutes, or until the pastry is golden brown and biscuity.

4. Meanwhile, lay out the second pastry sheet on a floured surface and cut out four 9cm pie tops.

5. Spoon the filling into the bases, brush the cooked pastry edges with beaten egg and top with the pie tops. Brush with beaten egg and make a small slit in the middle of each pie. Return the pies to the oven and bake for 30 minutes, or until golden.

RAW CHOCOLATE BBQ SAUCE
*VEGETARIAN *GLUTEN-FREE *DAIRY-FREE

You'll never buy a bottle of BBQ sauce again! My favourite way to serve this is at an Aussie sausage sizzle: barbecued sausages, crusty bread rolls and lots of sauce!

Makes about 600ml

1 tablespoon olive oil
2 garlic cloves, chopped
500g passata
3 tablespoons light agave syrup
6 tablespoons apple cider vinegar
4 tablespoons Worcestershire sauce
1 tablespoon Dijon mustard
1 tablespoon paprika
1 teaspoon ground ginger
1½ teaspoons raw cacao powder
Salt and pepper

1. Heat the oil in a saucepan over gentle heat, add the garlic and cook for 1–2 minutes until softened.

2. Stir in the remaining ingredients and season. Bring to the boil, then reduce the heat and simmer, uncovered, for 20–30 minutes, until thickened.

3. Store in an airtight container in the fridge for up to 2 weeks.

This sauce is all natural, contains no refined sugar and can be tailored to your own tastes. If you want it spicier, just add some chillies!

CAPONATA WITH CACAO

*VEGETARIAN *GLUTEN-FREE *DAIRY-FREE

This is a Sicilian classic but with an antioxidant chocolate twist. Make a big batch of it to accompany your meals all week. In my household, a favourite way to serve it is on top of scrambled eggs for extra protein, scattered with chopped basil and a pinch of chilli powder.

Serves 4

5 tablespoons olive oil
4 large aubergines (about 1kg), cut into 2cm dice
2 large red onions, halved and thinly sliced
400g cherry tomatoes, halved
60g capers, drained
60g raisins
60g green olives, stoned and quartered
4 celery sticks, cut into 2cm dice
1½ tablespoons rapadura (panela) or muscovado sugar
2 teaspoons dried chilli flakes
60ml red wine vinegar
2–3 teaspoons raw cacao powder
60g pine nuts, toasted
½ small bunch of basil, leaves picked, roughly chopped if large, to serve
Salt and pepper

1. Heat the oil in a wide saucepan over a medium heat and add the aubergines with a good sprinkle of salt and pepper. Cook for 15–20 minutes, or until soft. Remove and set aside.

2. Add a little more oil to the pan, heat, then add the onions and cook for about 5 minutes, or until soft and translucent. Add the aubergines back to the pan with the tomatoes and cook together for a further 5 minutes.

3. Add the capers, raisins, olives, celery, sugar, chilli flakes and vinegar, season well and cover with a lid. Cook over a low heat for 40 minutes, until all the vegetables are soft.

4. When the caponata is cooked, add the cacao powder and pine nuts, stirring them in gently so the stew doesn't break up too much. It should smell sweet and sour. Taste and adjust the seasoning, adding a little more sugar or a little more cacao, salt and pepper if needed.

5. Scatter the caponata with basil leaves to serve.

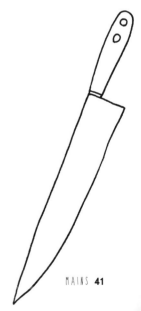

PORK MEATBALLS IN TOMATO SAUCE

This is my perfect mid-week go to. It's substantial and nourishing, yet still light with the homemade cherry tomato sauce. Finish it off with some raw cacao powder to add some depth and a touch of bitterness.

Serves 4

For the meatballs
500g pork mince
3 thyme sprigs, leaves picked
3 spring onions, finely chopped
1 egg
40g breadcrumbs
Olive oil, for frying
Salt and pepper

For the cherry tomato and chocolate sauce
1 tablespoon olive oil
2 garlic cloves, crushed
Pinch of dried chilli flakes
2 × 400g cans cherry tomatoes
2 teaspoons raw cacao powder
½ bunch of basil, leaves picked

To serve
400g seasonal greens, stalks removed chopped
Olive oil, for drizzling
30g Parmesan, shaved
Crusty sourdough bread

1. For the meatballs, put all the ingredients except the oil in a bowl. Season with salt and pepper, then use your hands to thoroughly mix everything together. Divide the mixture into 20 evenly sized pieces and roll each piece into a ball. Flatten the balls slightly so they will cook more quickly.

2. Heat the olive oil in a large frying pan over a medium heat then add the meatballs and fry for 5–6 minutes, turning once or twice, or until golden brown on both sides and cooked through.

3. In the meantime, for the sauce, heat the olive oil in a saucepan over a medium heat, add the garlic and the chilli flakes and fry for 1 minute. Tip in the tomatoes, increase the heat to high and simmer for 5 minutes to reduce slightly, then add the cacao powder and season with salt and pepper. Stir in the basil leaves, reserving a few for garnish.

4. Meanwhile, bring a large pot of water to the boil and cook the greens for 2–3 minutes. Drain, drizzle with olive oil and season.

5. Serve the meatballs with the sauce, shaved Parmesan, seasonal greens and some crusty sourdough bread.

Adding the raw cacao last ensures that it retains as much goodness as possible; make sure you don't overheat it.

CACAO & SPICE-RUBBED CHICKEN
*GLUTEN-FREE

Serve the chicken and roasted vegetables with all their juices on a platter, accompanied by all the fixings on the side. The perfect way to feed a crowd: everybody tucks in and shares the moment – it's what life's all about!

Serves 4–6

1 chicken (approx. 2kg)
2 sweet potatoes, peeled and cut into chunks
1 red and 1 yellow pepper, deseeded and cut into chunks
2 red onions, cut into wedges
2 tablespoons olive oil
2 avocados, peeled and stones removed, flesh scooped into small balls
Small bunch of coriander, leaves picked
1 lime, quartered
200g tub half-fat crème fraîche (optional)
Salt and pepper

For the rub
2–3 ancho or chipotle chillies (or use 1–2 tablespoons smoked paprika)
1 tablespoon cumin seeds
2 teaspoons dried oregano
2 garlic cloves
Pinch of celery salt
1 tablespoon olive oil
2 heaped teaspoons raw cacao powder
1 teaspoon dried chilli flakes

1. Preheat the oven to 180°C/gas mark 4.

2. In a pestle and mortar, grind all the rub ingredients together until you have a smooth paste. Set aside.

3. To spatchcock the chicken, flip it over so it is breast-side down, with the backbone facing you. Using a sturdy pair of kitchen or poultry scissors, cut down either side of the backbone, then remove and discard this. Turn the chicken over and push down firmly on the breastbone to flatten out the bird.

4. Put the vegetables on a baking tray, season with salt and pepper and drizzle with olive oil. Place the chicken on the bed of vegetables, then smear the rub over both the chicken and vegetables. Roast for 50–60 minutes, or until cooked through. Baste the chicken occasionally while it is cooking.

5. Serve the chicken, vegetables and cooking juices on a platter, with the avocado alongside, scattered with coriander and accompanied with lime wedges. It goes really well with crème fraîche on flatbreads.

FATTOUSH WITH FETA & RAW CHOCOLATE

*VEGETARIAN

A classic Middle Eastern salad with a twist – a final sprinkling of sumac, raw cacao and fresh herbs enlivens the whole dish. This makes a perfect lunchbox filler.

Serves 4

4 mini wholemeal pitta breads
1 tablespoon olive oil
500g cherry tomatoes
3 small (or 1 large) cucumbers
2 Little Gem lettuce
Small bunch of flat-leaf
    parsley, roughly chopped
½ small bunch of mint, leaves
    picked and roughly chopped
100g radishes

For the dressing
1 red onion, thinly sliced
1 garlic clove, crushed
Juice of 1 lemon
1 tablespoon red wine vinegar
3 tablespoons good olive oil,
    plus extra to drizzle
1 teaspoon sumac, plus extra
    to sprinkle
½ teaspoon raw cacao powder,
    plus extra to sprinkle
Salt and pepper

To serve
150g Kalamata olives
100g long green pickled
    peppers
200g feta cheese

1. Preheat the oven to 200°C/ gas mark 6. Toss the pitta with the olive oil, then place on a baking tray and bake for about 15 minutes until crisp. Allow to cool slightly, then break into shards.

2. Meanwhile, make the dressing. Put the onion and garlic in a small bowl and add the lemon juice, vinegar, oil, sumac and cacao powder. Season and mix well, then leave to infuse until the salad is finished.

3. Quarter the cherry tomatoes, roughly chop the cucumbers and larger lettuce leaves and put into a bowl. Add the herbs to the salad.

4. Toss the dressing with the salad, then, just before serving, cut the radishes into quarters and use to top the salad, along with the pitta bread and a sprinkle of sumac and cacao powder.

5. Serve the salad with the Kalamata olives, long green pickled peppers and feta cheese on the side.

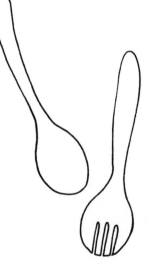

DESSERTS

WALNUT BAKLAVA *VEGETARIAN
WITH CACAO SYRUP

Walnuts are considered the king of the nut world and contain several unique and powerful antioxidants, including juglone, tellimagrandin and morin, which aid brain health. Pistachios are one of the oldest and most commonly used nuts in the world; their health benefits include promoting a healthy heart and improved digestion. Baklava will keep for several days in an airtight container – and arguably gets better over time.

Makes 20–30 diamonds

For the baklava
250g walnuts, roughly chopped
150g pistachios, roughly chopped
1 teaspoon ground cinnamon
1 packet filo pastry
60g butter, melted, plus extra for greasing
20–30 whole cloves

For the syrup
200g honey
200ml hot water
20g raw cacao powder
1 teaspoon instant coffee
1 cinnamon stick

1. Preheat the oven to 160°C/gas mark 3. Grease a 25 × 20cm baking tin.

2. To make the syrup, put all the ingredients in a saucepan and simmer for 5–10 minutes until the mixture has thickened slightly. Set aside.

3. For the baklava, blitz the walnuts and pistachios in a food-processor until reduced to a fine crumb consistency. Add the cinnamon, then set aside.

4. Cut the filo pastry sheets to size to fit your tin (you'll probably need to cut them in half). Brush a pastry sheet with melted butter and top with another sheet, then place in the tin. Add a layer of mixed nuts, top with a pastry sheet, brush with melted butter and top with another pastry sheet. Add another layer of nuts, then continue until you have used all the filo pastry and nuts, finishing with two pastry sheets. Brush again with melted butter, then score the top diagonally to create a diamond pattern.

5. Place a whole clove in each diamond. Cook for 45–60 minutes, until golden.

6. Leave the baklava to cool for a few minutes, then pour over the syrup. Let it soak for at least 2 hours before serving, but the longer the better.

Allow plenty of time for the syrup to work its way between the layers of pastry and nuts. The end result shouldn't be dry; rather, it should be a syrup-soaked raw chocolate once-in-a-while treat that still has a nutty crunch.

CACAO & PECAN
TAMALES *VEGETARIAN

Tamales are steamed parcels of corn dough wrapped in corn husks or leaves such as plantain or banana. They are traditionally savoury, but here I have made them sweet using chocolate with a hint of chilli and filled them with more chocolate and pecans. Dip them in Cacao Honey Sauce (see page 57) for extra indulgence.

Makes 10–12

For the tamale mixture
10–12 corn husks, 15 × 25cm pieces of greaseproof paper, or banana or plantain leaves, plus extra for lining the steamer
200g Mexican masa harina flour or cornmeal (polenta)
1 tablespoon raw cacao powder
2 teaspoons baking powder
1 teaspoon ground cinnamon
Pinch of chilli powder
Pinch of sea salt
About 350ml warm water
60g butter, softened
100g rapadura (panela) or muscovado sugar

For the chocolate pecan filling
100g raw chocolate (80 per cent cacao), finely chopped
50g pecan nuts, chopped
10g rapadura (panela) or muscovado sugar
30g butter, softened
½ teaspoon dried chilli flakes

1. Soak the corn husks or banana or plantain leaves in a bowl of warm water.

2. In a separate bowl, mix the masa harina or cornmeal, cacao powder, baking powder, cinnamon, chilli powder and salt. Gradually add enough warm water to bring everything together, mixing well, until you have a thick, spoonable paste. Rest for a few minutes, then mix in the butter and sugar. Set aside.

3. Mix together the filling ingredients into a crunchy paste.

4. Drain the corn husks or leaves and place flat on a surface with the pointed ends facing away from you (or the greaseproof paper with the short ends facing you). Spoon 2 tablespoons of the tamale mixture along the centre of each and spread out slightly. Place 1 tablespoon of chocolate pecan filling in the centre of each. Fold the sides in, flatten

down, then fold the tops down and the bottoms up to create a parcel. Tie securely with kitchen string, making sure that none of the dough is exposed.

5. Line a steamer basket with spare husks, leaves or paper. Fill a pot with water, ensuring that it doesn't touch the steamer. Cover and bring to the boil. Stand the tamales upright in the steamer, not packing too tightly. Steam the tamales for 45–55 minutes, checking the pan occasionally and adding water as needed.

6. To see if the tamales are ready, remove one from the steamer and peel back some of the wrapping: when cooked, it should be tender but solid, not mushy, and the wrapping should peel away easily. When cooked, let the steamer basket stand on a plate for 8 minutes to cool before serving.

COCONUT CREAM PANNA COTTA

*GLUTEN-FREE *DAIRY-FREE

These work equally well served in small glasses if you prefer, with no unmoulding necessary. Coconut milk is highly nutritious, rich in fibre and vitamins. Don't forget the antioxidant benefits of raw cacao either, which has abundant amounts of magnesium and other phytochemicals.

Serves 6

4 × 160ml cans coconut cream, stirred to combine the solids with the liquid
50g honey
40g raw chocolate (80 per cent cacao)
Zest of 1 lime
1 teaspoon vanilla paste
4 gelatine leaves

To serve
3 passion fruits, halved
12 lychees (optional)

1. Combine the coconut cream, honey, chocolate, lime zest and vanilla paste in a saucepan and heat very gently. Strain through a fine sieve.

2. Meanwhile, put the gelatine leaves in a bowl of cold water to soften for 4 minutes. Remove the gelatine from the water, squeeze to remove the excess water and then stir the gelatine into the warm coconut chocolate mixture until dissolved.

3. Divide the mixture among six dariole moulds or ramekins and leave to set in the fridge for at least 2 hours, preferably overnight.

4. When ready to serve, briefly dip each of the moulds into hot water to loosen, then turn out onto serving plates. Add half a passion fruit and two lychees (if using) to each plate and serve.

COCONUT RUM CACAO MOUSSE

*VEGETARIAN *GLUTEN-FREE *DAIRY-FREE

A dairy- and egg-free mousse that is good for you – pimped up with coconut rum. This guilt-free dessert uses a combination of avocado, raw chocolate and coconut milk for a nutrition overload: avocados are very high in potassium, which supports healthy blood pressure levels – it is an important mineral and most people don't get enough of it.

Serves 4–6

3 ripe Hass avocados, peeled and stones removed
30g raw cacao powder
80ml maple syrup
4 tablespoons coconut oil, melted
1 teaspoon vanilla extract
30ml coconut rum
400ml can coconut milk, chilled

To serve
A handful of unsweetened coconut flakes, toasted
200g fresh cherries

1. Put the avocado flesh, cacao powder, maple syrup, coconut oil, vanilla extract and coconut rum into a food-processor and blend until smooth.

2. Scoop out the chilled top portion of the coconut milk (the cream), leaving the water in the bottom, and put the cream into a bowl. Beat the coconut cream on a high setting for about 30 seconds, but no longer or the cream will split.

3. Mix the avocado and coconut creams together until blended completely, then divide among four or six ramekins. Leave to set in the fridge for a minimum of 2 hours.

4. Serve with toasted coconut flakes and cherries.

LOUKOUMADES & CACAO HONEY SAUCE

VEGETARIAN

The simplest things in life are often the best. These little fried balls of batter are dredged in sugar and cinnamon and raw cacao powder then dipped in a chocolate and honey sauce.

Serves 4–6

For the loukoumades
250g plain flour
1 tablespoon rapadura (panela) or muscovado sugar
1 tablespoon fast-action dried yeast
¼ teaspoon salt
¼ teaspoon freshly ground nutmeg
Vegetable oil, for frying

For the cacao honey sauce
140g raw chocolate (80 per cent cacao), chopped
70g honey
50g unsalted butter
Small pinch of salt

To finish
1 teaspoon ground cinnamon
1 teaspoon raw cacao powder
50g caster sugar

1. For the loukoumades, sift the flour into a large mixing bowl, add the sugar, dried yeast, salt and nutmeg. Gradually add 250ml of lukewarm water, stirring, until the mixture is smooth and slightly frothy. Cover and leave it in a warm place for about 1 hour, or until the mixture has doubled in volume and looks frothy.

2. When this batter is about ready, make the sauce. Melt the chocolate with the honey, butter and salt in a bain-marie (a heatproof bowl placed over a pan of simmering water), stirring frequently. Set aside.

3. Mix the cinnamon and cacao powder into the caster sugar. Set aside.

4. Meanwhile, heat the oil in a deep saucepan or deep-fat fryer, until very hot but not smoking. Using 1 teaspoon, dipped in water to prevent the mixture sticking to it, drop a teaspoon of the batter into the hot oil. Cook about 6–8 of these doughnut puffs at a time, depending on the size of your fryer. The loukoumades will puff up and rise to the top of the oil very quickly. Turn them over and, as they turn golden, remove them from the oil using a slotted spoon and place on kitchen paper to remove any excess oil. Repeat with the remainder of the batter.

5. While they are still warm, sprinkle the loukoumades with the sugar mixture. Serve drizzled with the chocolate honey sauce. Loukoumades are best eaten warm, on the same day they are made.

BANANA & CACAO
ICE CREAM

This potassium- and magnesium-fuelled fuss-free ice cream is a great way to use up those left over ripe bananas. It can also be added to your smoothies or an iced coffee.

Serves 4

6 bananas, peeled and sliced
1 teaspoon raw cacao
  powder, or to taste
10g raw cacao nibs

1. Put the bananas in an airtight container or freezer bag and freeze for at least 2 hours, ideally overnight.

2. Blend the frozen banana slices in a small food-processor or powerful blender. At first, the banana slices will look crumbly, then oatmealy. Keep blending, scraping down the sides of the food-processor or blender occasionally, until the mixture is creamy and there are no bits of banana left. Blend for a few more seconds to aerate the ice cream, then mix in the cacao powder.

3. Transfer to an airtight container and freeze until solid, then sprinkle over the cacao nibs. Freeze for at least another 2 hours before serving. It will keep in the freezer for up to 2 months.

DOUBLE CHOCOLATE CRACKLE COOKIES

*VEGETARIAN

A decadent rich chocolate cookie that is pretty and simple to make. Serve with scoops of nutritious Banana & Cacao Ice Cream (opposite).

Makes 16

150g plain flour
30g raw cacao powder
1 teaspoon baking powder
200g caster sugar
60g unsalted butter, chilled
  and diced
20g raw cacao nibs
2 eggs, lightly beaten
1 teaspoon vanilla extract

For the crackle topping:
50g icing sugar
50g raw cacao powder

1. Sift the flour, cacao powder, baking powder and caster sugar into a large bowl. Rub the butter into the flour mixture with your fingertips until it clumps together and resembles coarse breadcrumbs, then stir in the cacao nibs.

2. Whisk together the eggs and vanilla extract, then add to the flour mixture. Mix until combined, then cover and allow to rest for 30 minutes.

3. Meanwhile, preheat the oven to 190°C/gas mark 5 and line two baking trays with greaseproof paper.

4. For the crackle topping, sift the icing sugar and cacao powder into a bowl. Shape the cookie dough into walnut-sized balls and drop into the crackle topping mixture, tossing until well coated. Place on the lined baking trays, leaving space for the cookies to spread. Bake for 10–12 minutes, or until just set when lightly touched.

5. Transfer to a wire rack to cool.

BITTER CACAO JELLIES WITH YOGURT CREAM

These jellies, which are best served in small individual espresso size cups or jelly moulds, are punchy with strong chocolate and amaretto flavours – ideal for a nightcap.

Serves 6–8

For the jellies
50g raw cacao powder,
   plus extra to dust
150g rapadura (panela) or
   muscovado sugar
60ml Amaretto
1 teaspoon vanilla paste
7 gelatine leaves

For the yogurt cream
300ml double cream
150g Greek-style yogurt
Seeds from ½ vanilla pod
1 tablespoon icing sugar,
   or to taste

Fresh raspberries, to serve

1. For the jellies, put the cacao powder, sugar, Amaretto and vanilla paste in a saucepan with 500ml of water and bring to the boil over a medium heat.

2. Meanwhile, put the gelatine leaves in a bowl of cold water to soften for 4 minutes. Remove the gelatine from the water, squeeze to remove excess water, then add the gelatine to the hot chocolate mixture and stir to dissolve.

3. Divide the mixture among 6-8 small cups or glasses or individual jelly moulds and refrigerate for 3-4 hours, or until set.

4. For the yogurt cream, put the double cream, yogurt, vanilla seeds and icing sugar in a bowl and whisk together until soft peaks form.

5. To serve, unmould the jellies onto individual serving plates (briefly dip the moulds into hot water to loosen them if necessary), spoon over the yogurt cream, dust with cacao powder and serve with fresh raspberries.

KLADDKAKA *VEGETARIAN

A Swedish sticky, dense and chocolatey cake with a soft and gooey centre. A perfect kladdkaka is very soft in the middle, but not too runny once cooled.

Serves 8

2 eggs
225g golden caster sugar
1 teaspoon vanilla extract
100g plain flour
40g raw cacao powder, plus extra to serve
100g unsalted butter, melted, plus extra for greasing
Whipped cream mixed with vanilla paste, to serve (optional)

1. Preheat the oven to 180°C/gas mark 4. Grease and line a loose-bottomed 20cm round cake tin.

2. Whisk the eggs, sugar and vanilla extract together using a handheld electric mixer for 3–4 minutes until light, fluffy and pale.

3. Sift the flour and cacao powder into the egg and sugar mixture, then fold in carefully until everything is incorporated. Next, fold in the melted butter until you have a smooth, thick chocolatey mixture. Pour the cake batter into the lined tin and bake for about 15–20 minutes.

4. Remove from the oven and allow to cool until the middle has firmed up slightly. Serve with some whipped cream mixed with some vanilla paste and dusted with cacao powder, if you like.

The cake won't rise, but will puff up slightly during baking. If you press down gently on it the crust should crack. This signals that the cake is done.

CACAO PUDDING
& MAPLE ICE CREAM

*VEGETARIAN

This tasty and gratifying dessert is so straightforward to make. It oozes with a rich chocolate sauce, which pairs well with a scoop of your homemade maple ice cream. The addition of arrowroot powder to the dairy-free ice cream boosts the metabolism, increases circulation, reduces blood pressure, and promotes a healthy digestive system.

Serves 4

For the ice cream
2 × 400ml cans coconut milk
3 tablespoons arrowroot powder
2 teaspoons vanilla extract
60ml maple syrup
80g pecans, chopped

For the pudding
125g plain flour
Pinch of salt
220g rapadura (panela) or muscovado sugar
1 tablespoon baking powder
4 tablespoons raw cacao powder, plus 2 tablespoons for the topping
220ml almond milk
85g unsalted butter, melted
2 eggs, lightly beaten
1 teaspoon vanilla extract
1 tablespoon instant coffee or espresso powder diluted with 2 tablespoons just-boiled water
250ml boiling water

1. To make the ice cream, put the coconut milk and arrowroot powder in a saucepan and heat over a medium heat, stirring frequently, until it starts to boil and thicken. Set aside to cool for 5 minutes, then stir in the vanilla extract. Allow to cool completely.

2. Stir in the maple syrup and process in an ice-cream maker. Stir through the pecans. Freeze the ice cream in a freezable container for 3–4 hours.

3. For the pudding, preheat the oven to 180°C/gas mark 4.

4. Sift the flour, salt, 120g of the sugar, the baking powder and the cacao powder into a large bowl. Add the almond milk, melted butter, beaten eggs, vanilla extract and coffee mixture and mix using a handheld electric mixer until combined. Pour into a 1-litre baking dish.

5. Stir the remaining 100g of sugar and the remaining 2 tablespoons cacao powder together in a bowl, then sprinkle this over the pudding batter. Pour the boiling water carefully and gently over the pudding, then bake for 20–25 minutes. When the pudding is ready it will be firm with a slight wobble and a crusty top. The sauce will be hiding underneath as a little surprise!

6. Serve this oozy chocolate pudding with the maple and pecan ice cream.

RAW DATE, FIG & BLACKBERRY CAKE

*VEGETARIAN *GLUTEN-FREE *DAIRY-FREE

An impressive no-bake cake, with no refined sugar, dairy or gluten, which is very simple to make. The delicately flavoured cashew nut is celebrated here, packed with soluble dietary fibre, vitamins, minerals and numerous health-promoting phytochemicals that help protect from diseases and cancers. And it's not just a cake for vegans – everyone can enjoy it!

Serves 8

For the base
150g walnuts
200g pitted dates
6 tablespoons coconut oil

For the cake
400g cashews
4 tablespoons raw cacao powder
Juice of 1 lemon
100g pitted dates
100g soft dried figs
50g coconut oil
6 tablespoons maple syrup
1 teaspoon vanilla paste
About 100ml coconut water, adding enough until you have the right consistency
1 punnet (approx. 150g) blackberries, a few reserved for decorating

To serve
4 fresh figs, quartered
Rose petals (optional)

1. To make the base, blitz the walnuts into a fine crumb in a food-processor. Add the dates and keep processing until it all starts to stick together, before adding the coconut oil. Press into the bottom of a 20cm spring-form cake tin, or adjustable tin. Refrigerate to allow it to set for a few hours.

2. To make the cake, start by soaking the cashews in hot water for 30 minutes. Drain the cashews and put them into a food-processor. Add the cacao powder, lemon juice, dates, figs, coconut oil, maple syrup and vanilla paste and blend together. Keeping the motor running, gradually add the coconut water and blend until the mixture is of cake-batter consistency – smooth, thick and creamy. This may take up to 5 minutes.

3. Pour over the base, then gently stir through the blackberries, reserving a few for decoration. Smooth the top and let it set overnight, or for at least 12 hours, in the fridge.

4. Serve topped with the reserved blackberries, the quartered figs and rose petals (if using).

Cashews' small small amount of zeaxanthin also provides antioxidant and protective UV filtering functions.

CACAO &
CARDAMOM BUNS
*VEGETARIAN

As well as having aromatic qualities, cardamom is rich in many vital vitamins for optimum health. Rapadura (panela) sugar is higher than other sugars in several essential minerals, including potassium, magnesium and phosphorus, making this recipe good for the heart and soul!

*Makes 7 large or
9 smaller buns*

300ml whole milk
10g raw cacao powder
1 teaspoon ground
  cardamom
50g butter, plus extra
  for greasing
425g strong bread flour,
  plus extra for dusting
7g fast-action dried yeast
80g caster sugar
1 egg, lightly beaten
A little beaten egg,
  for glazing

For the filling
75g butter, softened
50g rapadura (panela) or
  muscovado sugar, plus
  extra for sprinkling
30g raw cacao powder

1. In a small saucepan, bring the milk, cacao powder and cardamom to just below the boil. Take off the heat, stir in the butter and leave to infuse until just warm.

2. Meanwhile, in a large bowl, sift together the flour, yeast and sugar. When the milk mix is just warm, make a well in the middle of the dry ingredients and add the beaten egg. Stir in, then strain in the milk and stir together to make a soft dough that comes away from the sides of the bowl.

3. Tip the dough onto a lightly oiled work surface and knead for 5 minutes. Then return the dough to the bowl, cover and leave somewhere warm to prove for 30 minutes.

5. While the dough is proving, make the filling by beating together the butter, sugar and cacao powder until soft and easily

spreadable. Grease a 23cm round cake tin.

6. Roll the dough out on a lightly floured surface to a rectangle roughly 35 × 25cm. Spread the filling over the dough, then, starting from one of the long edges, roll the dough up tightly like a Swiss roll. Position it on its seam, and cut into seven or nine slices.

7. Arrange the slices in the tin, cut side up and evenly spaced out, with the smallest in the middle. Cover and leave to prove for about 30 minutes, until the dough springs back when prodded gently. Meanwhile, preheat the oven to 200°C/gas mark 6.

8. Brush the top of the slices with a little beaten egg and sprinkle with sugar. Bake for 25 minutes, or until golden brown. Serve warm.

WALNUT, CACAO & LIQUORICE TART
*VEGETARIAN

Chocolate and liquorice are a really great pairing! The subtle sweetness of the liquorice goes well with the bitterness and richness of the raw chocolate, baked in buttery and crumbly short walnut and cacao nib pastry. Liquorice in its root form is known for its anti-viral anti-oxidant, anti-spasmodic and antidepressant activities.

Serves 8–10

For the walnut and cacao nib pastry
225g plain flour, plus extra
  for dusting
100g butter, chilled, diced
50g walnuts, finely chopped
30g raw cacao nibs
Pinch of salt
1 egg, lightly beaten

For the filling
300g raw chocolate
  (80 per cent cacao),
  roughly chopped
2 eggs
250ml double cream
60ml liquorice syrup
  (see note right)

Whipped cream, to serve

1. To make the pastry, sift the flour into a large bowl, and rub in the butter with your fingertips until the mixture resembles fine breadcrumbs. Stir in the walnuts, cacao nibs and salt, then add the egg and 1-2 tablespoons of water and mix to a firm dough. Knead the dough briefly and gently on a floured surface, then wrap in clingfilm and chill.

2. Preheat the oven to 190°C/ gas mark 5. Roll out the pastry to about 3mm thick, lay into a 25cm round tart tin and prick the base all over with a fork. Chill for 10 minutes.

3. Line the pastry with greaseproof paper, fill with ceramic baking beans, then bake for 10 minutes. Remove the beans and paper and bake for a further 4–5 minutes until just golden brown. Reduce the oven temperature to 110°C/gas mark ¼.

4. While the case is baking, make the filling. Melt the chocolate in a bain-marie (a heatproof bowl placed over a pan of simmering water). Lightly beat the eggs in a bowl. Gently heat the cream and liquorice syrup together and pour this over the eggs. Mix thoroughly, then pour over the melted chocolate. Stir together, then pour into the baked pastry case. Bake for 50 minutes.

5. Allow the cooked tart to cool, then serve with whipped cream.

To make your own liquorice syrup:
In a saucepan, gently heat 150g molasses, 200g chopped unsweetened soft natural liquorice bars, 5g aniseeds, 5g fennel seeds and 500ml water. Bring to a gentle boil and cook for 10 minutes or until thickened. Keep refrigerated for up to 2 weeks.

CACAO & ALMOND
DACQUOISE *VEGETARIAN

There's a lot to love about the combination of chocolate, almond and meringue! This cake keeps in the fridge for several days, making it an entertainer's make-ahead dream.

Serves 8

For the chocolate almond meringue
5 egg whites
Pinch of salt
275g golden caster sugar
100g ground almonds
1 teaspoon vanilla extract
40g raw cacao powder, sifted
30g raw cacao nibs

To finish
400ml double cream
50g light honey
1 teaspoon raw cacao powder
400g fresh mixed berries
A handful of flaked almonds
2 teaspoons bee pollen

1. Preheat the oven to 150°C/gas mark 2.

2. For the meringue, in a clean, dry bowl, using a handheld electric mixer, whisk the egg whites with the pinch of salt until stiff. Gradually add the sugar, whisking constantly. Whisk for about 5 minutes, until the mixture is thick and glossy. Gently fold in the ground almonds, vanilla extract and cacao powder until just mixed through, to retain as much volume in the meringue as possible.

3. Line three baking trays with greaseproof paper and mark each paper with a 22cm circle. Spread the meringue onto the three circles using a spatula or palette knife. Top each meringue with a third of the cacao nibs.

4. Bake the meringues for 1 hour, or longer if necessary. They are cooked when their undersides are free of sticky patches. Turn the oven off and leave the meringues to cool in the oven with the door ajar.

5. Whip the cream, honey and cacao powder until soft peaks form, then set aside. Once the meringues have cooled, spread a third of the cream onto one of the meringues and top with a third of the mixed berries, then top with another meringue and repeat twice.

6. Sprinkle the top with flaked almonds and bee pollen. The end result will be a decadent tower of chocolatey meringues filled with cream and fruit – a luxurious dessert.

TREATS

DRIED FRUIT
& CACAO LOLLIPOPS

*VEGETARIAN *GLUTEN-FREE *DAIRY-FREE

Kids just love these – especially if they have been involved in making them. I always keep a stash in the fridge and offer them as an afternoon treat to friends when they pop round. You will need silicone lollipop moulds and lollipop sticks for the moulded lollipops, or alternatively, wooden sticks, a piping bag with a small plain tip and greaseproof paper for the 'chocolate lace' lollipops.

Makes 16 × 5cm diameter lollipops

200g raw chocolate buttons or raw chocolate (80 per cent cacao), broken into pieces
100g mixed dried fruit and nuts (e.g. raisins, goji berries, pumpkin seeds, almonds, unsweetened coconut flakes, freeze-dried strawberries or raspberries, sliced dried figs and bee pollen)

1. Melt the chocolate in a bain-marie (a heatproof bowl placed over a pan of simmering water), stirring occasionally.

For moulded lollipops
2. Put some dried fruit and nuts into each of the lollipop moulds, put the lollipop sticks into the moulds, then top with melted chocolate until the moulds are almost full. Smooth out with a knife if you need to. Top the chocolate-filled moulds with more dried fruit and nuts to make double-sided lollipops, arranging in the pattern of your choice.

3. Place in the fridge to set for an hour before serving.

For 'chocolate lace' lollipops
2. Using a glass as a template, draw circles on greaseproof paper, spacing them out. Fit a piping bag with a small plain tip, then fill the bag with the melted chocolate.

3. Place a lollipop stick on each circle with one end of the stick at the centre of the circle. Pipe overlapping lines of chocolate in swirls inside each circle. Scatter some dried fruit and nuts on top, then pipe a little more of the chocolate on top of the fruit and nuts so they are well attached.

4. Allow to set for 30 minutes in the fridge before carefully detaching the chocolate lollipops from the paper.

FRUIT & NUT BARK

*VEGETARIAN *GLUTEN-FREE *DAIRY-FREE

Vegan, gluten-free, grain-free, no bake/raw, refined sugar-free, soy-free! This homemade chocolate is made with just a few essential ingredients. You can also use any toppings you'd like – dried fruit, nuts and seeds all work well. It melts faster than traditional chocolate so it's best kept in the fridge or eat it straight from the freezer!

Serves 8–10

50g coconut oil, melted
50g raw cacao powder
1 tablespoon maple syrup
Pinch of sea salt
50g mixed dried vine fruit (e.g. raisins, currants, golden raisins, green raisins)
50g mixed nuts (e.g. shelled pistachios, pecans and almonds), roughly chopped

1. Line a small container with non-stick baking paper or clingfilm, about 25 × 15cm.

2. In a small bowl, gently stir together the melted coconut oil, cacao powder and maple syrup until completely smooth. Add the pinch of sea salt and combine well, then taste and add more maple syrup if desired. Stir in the dried fruit and nuts.

3. Pour the chocolate mixture into the lined container and spread out evenly using the back of a spoon to a thickness of 1cm so the fruit and nuts are in one layer. Place the container flat in the freezer for up to 30 minutes, until the chocolate is completely hard.

4. Break up into pieces and serve immediately. Store in the freezer.

CACAO BARS

Raw cacao is a mood enhancer. It increases serotonin and affects other neurotransmitters, which make us feel happy. Chocolate making is very quick and easy: anyone can do it and kids love it. The basics are simply grated cacao butter, raw cacao powder, coconut oil and a natural sweetener. I have suggested some flavour combinations in the following recipes, but do enjoy making up your own.

Serves 8–10

170g cacao butter
100g coconut oil, plus extra
   for greasing
170g raw cacao powder
60g light agave syrup

*For the Chilli and
Peppercorn Bars*
1–2 teaspoons dried chilli
   flakes
1–2 teaspoons pink
   peppercorns, lightly
   crushed
1 large pinch of Angel Hair
   chilli (or use a mellow
   smoked chilli, e.g. mulato)

For the Raspberry Bars
100g freeze-dried
   raspberries (or use
   strawberries)
1 tablespoon raspberry
   powder

CHILLI & PEPPERCORN BARS

1. Line a 23 × 13cm loaf tin or six mini 13.5 × 6.5 × 4cm loaf tins with clingfilm and grease with coconut oil. Melt the cacao butter and coconut oil in a bain-marie (a heatproof bowl placed over a pan of simmering water), stirring occasionally.

2. Add the cacao powder to the bowl of melted oil and butter and stir until smooth. Stir in the agave syrup, adjusting the amount to your taste.

3. Mix in half the chilli flakes until well combined. Pour the chocolate mixture into the prepared loaf tin. Top with the remaining chilli flakes, the pink peppercorns and angel hair chilli. Place in the freezer for 30 minutes, or in the fridge for 1 hour, before serving.

RASPBERRY BARS

1. Follow the method above for steps 1 and 2.

2. Mix in half the freeze-dried raspberries and half the raspberry powder until well combined. Pour the chocolate mixture into the prepared mini loaf tins. Top with the remaining freeze-dried raspberries and raspberry powder. Place in the freezer for 30 minutes, or in the fridge for 1 hour, before serving.

HAZELNUT & CACAO PRALINE

*VEGETARIAN *GLUTEN-FREE *DAIRY-FREE

The flavour combination of chocolate and hazelnut never disappoints. As well as being delicious, these little bites pack a punch in the health department. With a robust amount of vitamin E, hazelnuts contribute to maintaining healthy skin and hair by improving moisture and elasticity. Its antioxidant capabilities can help prevent damage from UV and external free radicals.

Makes 24

200g raw chocolate (80 per cent cacao), broken into pieces
100g hazelnut butter
3 tablespoons maple syrup
30g coconut oil
20g raw cacao powder
½ teaspoon vanilla paste
Pinch of salt
50g roasted hazelnuts, chopped

1. Melt the chocolate in a bain-marie (a heatproof bowl placed over a pan of simmering water), stirring occasionally. Set aside.

2. In a bowl, mix together the hazelnut butter, maple syrup, coconut oil, cacao powder, vanilla paste and salt until well combined, then stir in half the melted chocolate. Leave to set in the fridge for at least an hour.

3. Line a baking tray with greaseproof paper. Form the chilled chocolate mixture into 24 × 1.5–2cm balls and place on the prepared baking tray. Transfer to the freezer to set for 30 minutes.

4. Re-melt the remaining chocolate then, using a fork, dip each ball into the chocolate and place in a mini cupcake case. Top with the chopped hazelnuts while the chocolate is still soft. Refrigerate until ready to serve.

CACAO-COATED KIRSCH CHERRIES

*VEGETARIAN *GLUTEN-FREE *DAIRY-FREE

Tossing and turning at night? Cherries to the rescue! Cherries are a good source of melatonin, which helps us regulate our sleep cycle. These sweet bites would be the perfect ending to a dinner party or a great little nightcap after a night out.

Makes 24

150ml kirsch
30g agave syrup or honey
24 fresh cherries, stems attached but stones removed
200g raw chocolate (80 per cent cacao), broken into pieces

1. Start this recipe the night before by gently heating the kirsch and agave syrup or honey in a saucepan. Place the cherries with the stalks upwards in the pan and allow to heat gently but not boil for 10 minutes. Remove from the heat and leave to cool and steep overnight.

2. Melt the chocolate in a bain-marie (a heatproof bowl placed over a pan of simmering water), stirring occasionally.

3. Remove the cherries from the liquid and drain on kitchen paper. Line a baking tray with greaseproof paper.

4. Once the cherries are dry, dip them into the melted chocolate and place onto the prepared baking tray. Place in the fridge until set. They will keep in an airtight container in the fridge for 2–3 days.

PEANUT BUTTER TRUFFLES

*VEGETARIAN *GLUTEN-FREE *DAIRY-FREE

Serve these as a truffle treat or have one with a cup of tea as a pick-me-up in the afternoon. The addition of peanuts is a good source of dietary protein, composed of fine quality amino acids that are essential for growth and development.

Makes 20

100g smooth peanut butter
45g ground almonds
50g rapadura (panela) or muscovado sugar
120g raw chocolate (80 per cent cacao), broken into pieces

1. Mix the peanut butter and ground almonds together in a mixing bowl. Gradually stir in the sugar until well combined into a dough ball. Cover the bowl tightly with clingfilm and refrigerate for at least 1 hour until ready to use.

2. Divide and shape the dough into 20 × 1.5–2cm balls and place on a baking tray. Cover and refrigerate for at least 20 minutes to firm up. Line a second baking tray with greaseproof paper.

3. Melt the chocolate in a bain-marie (a heatproof bowl placed over a pan of simmering water), stirring occasionally.

4. Dip the peanut butter balls, one at a time, into the melted chocolate, allowing the excess to drip off. Place on the lined baking tray, cover and refrigerate until ready to serve. They will keep in an airtight container in the fridge for up to 1 week.

HOT CHOCOLATE

*VEGETARIAN *GLUTEN-FREE

This recipe works brilliantly served warm with a dollop of Banana & Cacao Ice Cream (see page 58) on top. Alternatively, allow to cool and serve with ice.

Serves 1

250ml whole milk or
   almond milk
1 tablespoon raw cacao
   powder
1 teaspoon honey

Flavourings (optional)
3 cardamom pods, bruised
   and seeds removed
Pinch of dried chilli flakes
Cinnamon stick

Place all the ingredients into a saucepan with your choice of flavourings, if using, and heat gently without boiling for 4–5 minutes. Pour into a mug and enjoy.

To make this
dairy-free, you can
use any nut milk.
I prefer almond milk,
but cashew or hazelnut
also work.

CACAO MARTINI

*VEGETARIAN *GLUTEN-FREE *DAIRY-FREE

This naughty but nice Martini is perfect for chocolate lovers! Frangelico is made from toasted wild hazelnuts found only in the north of Italy, which are combined with cocoa, vanilla berries and a host of other natural extracts to make up this complex flavoured liqueur.

Serves 2

Crushed ice
2 teaspoons raw cacao
   powder
2 teaspoons agave syrup,
   or to taste
120ml Frangelico
200ml vodka
1 teaspoon vanilla extract

To serve
Raw cacao powder
A few raw cacao nibs

1. Chill two glasses with crushed ice. Dissolve the cacao powder in about 2 tablespoons of warm water and mix in the agave syrup. Put into a cocktail shaker, add the Frangelico, vodka and vanilla extract and shake for 20 seconds.

2. Tip the ice out of the glass and pour in the contents of the cocktail shaker. Decorate with a little cacao powder and a few cacao nibs and serve.

INDEX

SOURCES

Here are some useful websites for buying raw chocolate:

www.therawchocolatecompany.com
www.therawchocolateshop.com
www.consciouschocolate.com
www.enjoyrawchocolate.com
www.amazon.co.uk
www.buywholefoodsonline.co.uk
www.ocado.co.uk

ACKNOWLEDGEMENTS

The hugest thank you to all at Kyle Books and especially Claire Rogers. Thank you Faith Mason for your gorgeous photography and Jacqui Mellville for lovely props! The perfect creative team!

The biggest thank you goes to Sarah Fassnidge for being the best assistant ever and my recipe testing team; India Whiley-Morton, Kitty Coles and Sarah Fassnidge. Thank you to Jenni Desmond for the illustrations which brought the pages to life!

Thank you to my family and friends all over the globe; Greece, Australia and UK. Without you this would not be possible. Thank you most Matthew x

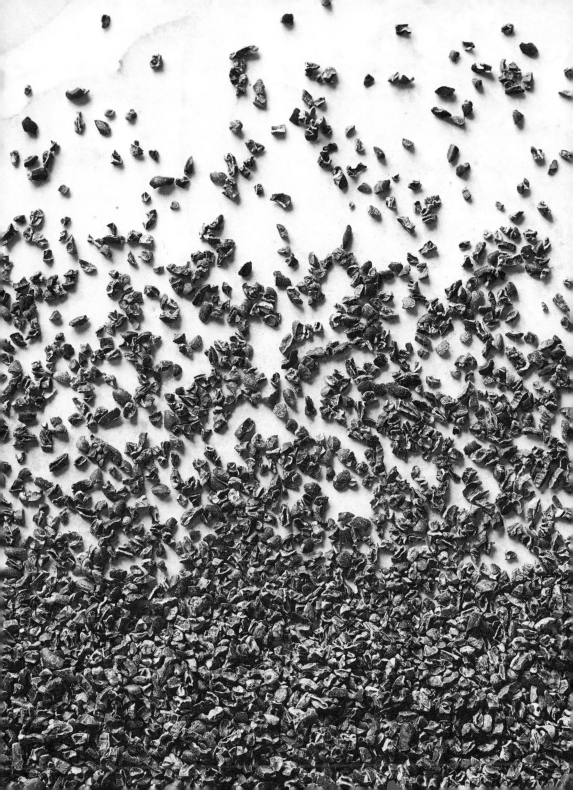

First published in Great Britain in 2017 by
Kyle Books, an imprint of Kyle Cathie Ltd
192–198 Vauxhall Bridge Road
London SW1V 1DX
general.enquiries@kylebooks.com
www.kylebooks.co.uk

10 9 8 7 6 5 4 3 2 1

ISBN 978 0 85783 412 6

Project Editor: Claire Rogers
Copy Editor: Anne McDowall
Proofreader: Anne Sheasby
Designer: Helen Bratby
Photographer: Faith Mason
Illustrator: Jenni Desmond
Food Stylist: Kathy Kordalis
Food Stylist's Assistant: Sarah Fassnidge
Recipe Testers: Sarah Fassnidge, India
    Whiley-Morton and Kitty Coles
Prop Stylist: Jacqui Melville
Production: Nic Jones and Gemma John

A Cataloguing in Publication record
for this title is available from the British
Library.

Colour reproduction by ALTA London
Printed and bound in China by C&C Offset
Printing Co., Ltd.

* Note: all eggs are medium free-range